Around the World

Food Around the World

By Meg Gaertner

level 2 little blue readers

www.littlebluehousebooks.com

Little Blue House is distributed by North Star Editions:
sales@northstareditions.com | 888-417-0195

Produced for Little Blue House by Red Line Editorial.

Photographs ©: iStockphoto, cover, 4, 7, 8–9, 10, 12–13, 15, 16–17, 18, 20–21, 23, 24 (top left), 24 (top right), 24 (bottom left), 24 (bottom right)

Library of Congress Control Number: 2020900858

ISBN
978-1-64619-183-3 (hardcover)
978-1-64619-217-5 (paperback)
978-1-64619-285-4 (ebook pdf)
978-1-64619-251-9 (hosted ebook)

Printed in the United States of America
Mankato, MN
082020

About the Author

Meg Gaertner enjoys reading, writing, dancing, and being outside. Her favorite foods include sushi, chicken tikka masala, and anything with chocolate in it. She lives in Minnesota.

Table of Contents

Many Types of Food

People around the world eat different foods.

Some people eat a mix of meat and corn. The mix is cooked inside a dry leaf.

corn
meat

Many people around
the world eat a hot pie.
The pie is filled with meat.

bread

Bread and Rice

Many people eat bread. Some people put small bits of fruit in their bread.

Some people eat flatbread. They eat it with their hands.

flatbread

Many people eat rice.
Some people eat it
with fish.

fish
rice

Other people eat rice with meat or vegetables.

rice
meat

cake

Sweets

Many people eat sweets. They eat cake or other treats.

Some people eat cookies. The cookies have a sweet filling in the middle.

cookie
filling

Some people eat a cold treat.
It comes in many different colors.

Glossary

bread

cookies

cake

rice

Index